# Tales from the Project Trade

By Paul F. Snare

© 2002 by Paul F. Snare. All rights reserved.

No part of this publication may be reproduced, stored in a retrieval system, or transmitted, in any form or by any means, electronic, mechanical, photocopying, recording, or otherwise, without the written prior permission of the author.

**National Library of Canada Cataloguing in Publication Data**

Snare, Paul, 1934-
    Tales from the project trade

ISBN 1-55369-164-4

    1. Project management. I. Title.

HD69.P75S53 2002        658.404        C2002-900269-9

# TRAFFORD

**This book was published *on-demand* in cooperation with Trafford Publishing.**
On-demand publishing is a unique process and service of making a book available for retail sale to the public taking advantage of on-demand manufacturing and Internet marketing. **On-demand publishing** includes promotions, retail sales, manufacturing, order fulfilment, accounting and collecting royalties on behalf of the author.

Suite 6E, 2333 Government St., Victoria, B.C. V8T 4P4, CANADA
Phone    250-383-6864        Toll-free   1-888-232-4444 (Canada & US)
Fax        250-383-6804        E-mail     sales@trafford.com
Website   www.trafford.com
TRAFFORD PUBLISHING IS A DIVISION OF TRAFFORD HOLDINGS LTD.
Trafford Catalogue #01-0566     www.trafford.com/robots/01-0566.html

10    9    8    7    6    5    4    3    2

# Acknowledgments

My thanks to Sonia Cole and Dona McAdam who helped convert my rough thoughts into the words of this book; and to my wife, Louise, whose support and tolerance of our often-separated lifestyle, allowed me to manage projects.

# Table of Contents

Introduction ...................... 7
Agendas ........................... 9
Arrogance ........................ 11
Assumptions ..................... 13
Bad news ........................ 17
Bonuses .......................... 19
Capital project systems ..... 21
Changing horses midstream 23
Check those shovels ......... 25
Cleverness ....................... 27
Common enemy .............. 29
Confidence ....................... 31
Confidentiality ................. 33
Constructability ............... 35
Contingency .................... 37
Cost management ............ 39
Delegation ....................... 41
Design documents ........... 43
Diversity .......................... 45
Education and training ..... 47
A few words .................... 49
Frankness ........................ 51
Goal setting ..................... 53
History ............................ 55

Hoopla ............................ 57
Issue and conflict resolution 59
Key numbers ................... 61
Learning never ends ......... 63
Loyalty and trust ............. 65
Mutual objectives ............ 67
Negotiating ..................... 69
Open listening ................. 71
Personal targets ............... 73
Planning .......................... 75
Plant staff on projects ....... 77
Procurement .................... 79
Project justification .......... 81
Project names .................. 83
Promotions ...................... 85
Providing help ................. 87
Review process ................ 89
Safety behavior ................ 91
Selection process ............. 93
Sexual harassment .......... 95
Solving problems ............. 97
Startup ............................ 99
Success factors ............... 101
Time .............................. 103

## Introduction

The president of a large, successful engineering and construction company once told me, "Having our people learn lessons from past projects is the most valuable thing we can do for our company." "But," he said, "we have not been able to do that effectively, nor am I familiar with any firm doing it even remotely well." My experience supports his view.

In the 1980s, the engineering group I was working with took a run at documenting and transferring lessons from past to future projects using a database. Trying to have new teams apply those lessons turned out to be a wasted effort. There were several reasons:

- Lessons reported were often symptoms of more basic underlying problems.
- Lessons stemming from behavioral issues were deemed too risky to report because in the next project, roles might be reversed and personal evaluations could suffer.
- Users of the data would respond with "I'm not that dumb!" or "My project's different."

A look at the research on the subject of capital projects reveals, not surprisingly, one interesting conclusion: what draws most people to project work is the enjoyment that comes from solving problems. I can testify that every project, when you live with it throughout its life, seems like one continuous problem, regardless of the outcome. There are project people who, if things are slow, will invent problems so they can display their problem-solving skills. Some would say that this argues against learning lessons to minimize problems. I would assert, however, that if a well-constructed program is introduced and answers positively the "What's in it for me?" question that all of us ask, then there should be positive results.

It is said that we learn best from our own mistakes. Yet, there are some useful lessons that we can learn from the experience of others that may help us prevent mistakes and missteps and thereby contribute to the success of a project. In this book, rather than provide an engineering approach to the principles, practices and procedures of project management, I describe my experiences and observations gathered during my career as a project manager. Instead of sorting everything into lists, categories and flow charts, I use real stories to illustrate the lessons.

Philip Crosby's book, *Quality is Free\** contains a wonderful phrase that encapsulates what project management is about: "It's not what you know, it's what you do about what you know." The stories in this book illustrate the "do" in that quotation.

By my definition, projects are temporary organizations established to achieve a specific set of objectives including cost, schedule, quality, performance and other measurements. There is an assigned team plus stakeholders, who may or may not influence the team but whose future is affected by the outcome of the project. The project is usually accomplished within a larger organization. Examples include running a political campaign, making a motion picture or building a chemical process installation.

Creating this book was also influenced by a question from our younger daughter. One evening while I was working on schedules, estimates and other papers covering our dining room table, she looked at me and asked, "How do you know what to do?" What a question! She used seven words to focus on the basics of project work: priority, allocation of time, skill, knowledge and the good judgment to do the right thing at the right time. I've never forgotten to periodically ask myself if I was doing the right thing and sometimes, more importantly, did I know what I was doing and how to do it?

According to a Persian proverb, One pound of learning requires ten pounds of common sense for its application. The successful project managers I know have a full toolbox of skills and the "perfect pitch" to be able to tune their efforts to accomplish what is required. I hope the material in this book adds practical and useful ideas to your toolbox.

---

\*Philip B. Crosby, *Quality is Free: The Art of Making Quality Certain*. New York: McGraw-Hill, 1979.

# Agendas...

Most of the projects I was involved with had a business or operations vice-president as the accountable manager. The corporation held this person responsible for the capital investment and its successful operation. The knowledge of what made capital projects successful varied widely among those accountable managers.

The project manager needs to discover the accountable manager's agenda. A cardinal rule is that the real agenda is what he is willing to spend time and money on. At the outset of one large project I was involved in, the accountable vice president said safety was his first priority. I had heard this from a number of senior managers in the past and, unfortunately, safety was not usually first when a situation tested the priority. However, on this project, the time and money directed at safety was exemplary. We later found out that there had been two fatalities at a plant he had managed. That experience made him a true believer in safety as a guiding value.

Sometimes there is an absence of any agenda. A project manager with a superior who has no knowledge of project management cannot ignore that situation. My solution is to find a project-competent person in the company whom the superior respects. Then, by direct or indirect means, get them to spend time together with the object of transferring knowledge about what makes a project successful. If you have a trusting relationship with the superior you can do the educating yourself but be aware that if the project gets into problems, you risk him concluding that you led him astray.

In my experience, the biggest risk to project success comes from making too many changes to the original plan. It works to have a respected senior manager explain to the vice-president accountable for the project that, as a project progresses, it is like an accelerating flywheel. The later changes are made the bigger and more lethal the wreck will be. The changes should stop.

## Arrogance...

The construction and engineering industry harbors some macho attitudes that are defended as necessary for getting things done. I have seen a change over the years toward a more open and understanding approach but some things still get in the way of some people and a few firms.

In the mid-80s, my company interviewed several contractors who were competing for a cost reimbursable contract worth $6 million. One contractor came to the interview with the top officers and several staff managers plus the person they proposed as the site manager. Their presentation took three hours. The president spoke for about an hour about the company's origins, financial strength and staff competency and described many of their successful projects. (Not too much was said about the ones that were not successes; someone else, he said, undid those.) The proposed site manager got ten minutes of airtime. The balance was filled with descriptions of home-office estimating and scheduling capabilities.

The contractor who succeeded in winning the contract showed up with only three people. The vice-president introduced the other two and said that the site manager would make the total presentation. In the beginning, I was only concerned about their jackets and ties. When the site manager shed his jacket, revealing a tattoo on his forearm, my fears lessened and then faded completely when he explained his practical and successful background. The presentation was centered on how the site team would function and be staffed. A bit of time was spent describing home office support. He asked me questions as part of his company's process to understand the client.

When I called the other contractor to tell them they didn't get the job, the vice president of business development asked to meet with me to learn why they were unsuccessful. I was happy to do that. In the meeting I laid out the reasons: spending little time addressing our specific project; dwelling on things not germane to choosing between contractors; not letting the site manager show his stuff; and never asking what our project objectives were. The presentation seemed like a major ego trip for the contractor's president and leaders and that told us all we needed to know.

The chosen contractor worked out well and demonstrated that customer satisfaction drives success in our industry. The project manager can use this thought-provoking example to judge how to treat the project's customers. You may think you know but without an exercise in identifying the customer's needs and their requirements, you are flying blind.

## Assumptions...

I learned several lessons during the Pampers startup in Cheboygan, Michigan. One, which sprang from an unexpected source, was about making assumptions.

The original production equipment was very touchy. It was a continuous challenge to get everything working in unison so that assembling the various raw materials would result in a carton of quality product to move to the warehouse. To identify problems, we kept logbooks at key points on the assembly line for operators and maintenance folks to record downtime events, probable causes, solutions and other observations that they thought would be helpful. The entries were summarized daily by a technician and distributed to supervisors for analysis and the creation of permanent solutions.

The results were generally good but we found an interesting and, at first, puzzling situation: one of the best maintenance mechanics rarely made an entry in the logbook. The initial reaction of some of the older supervisors was that he was keeping information from his co-workers to maintain his edge in knowledge and his reputation. Some thought he might have strong union feelings and was reluctant to share operating details with supervision that might help them during a strike.

Finally, one of the foremen took a chance and asked the mechanic why he didn't make entries in the logbook. His answer was simple: he felt he had lousy penmanship and was ashamed to have his writing on display. They worked out a system to have his entries typed prior to giving them to the technician who did the summaries.

There were two similar situations at different sites. At one, a packaging technician kept missing the color standard because he was colorblind. And at another, a ship's crane operator damaged rolls of paper when he loaded them because he was blind in one eye and lacked normal depth perception.

A manager I once worked with had supervised a production operation in Mexico. For him, a major challenge was to find well-motivated and technically aware people and then educate them in operations. He was responsible for the operation of two paper machines which were large, expensive and complicated mechanical monsters that needed a crew of six or seven people on each shift to keep them producing target tons of quality product.

One employee, who demonstrated the raw talent but had an attendance problem, caused my friend to intercede with mill management on several occasions. One morning the employee was absent for his day shift and my friend hit the roof. He started termination procedures and had the process moving ahead when, later that afternoon, he found out from the second shift foreman that the employee, because of absenteeism, had worked his day shift the prior day, as well as a full second shift, for a total of sixteen hours. He reversed the termination process and apologized to the employee when he next saw him. He also passed on this example in subsequent management meetings.

Another situation happened to me. We were installing a new wood chip delivery system to existing pulp digesters. The final construction push occurred during a three-week operations shutdown after which the new system would be running. This annual shutdown was normally two weeks but the paper business was slow at that time so a three-week downtime period was planned to minimize overtime costs and reduce inventory. In some unknown way that longer shutdown, in response to poor business conditions, translated in my brain as an assumption that nobody was concerned about a fast startup. I never published a startup curve that forecast daily output, starting low and increasing over time.

The first day after the shutdown we had wood chips everywhere, on the ground, on the floor, on the roof. A few made it into the digesters and with time, attention and some dedicated effort, the system finally worked. My reputation deservedly suffered from my lack of foresight. Also, I did not provide for enough people to reprogram the computer logic. Our only process control engineer was overloaded as we started up and we had to shut down the remedial work while he got some sleep.

The lessons — and they have been relearned often — are that speculation is not a substitute for original data obtained by asking questions, and that assumptions (e.g., everyone will write in the logbook) are not always correct. Walk around, look, ask questions. Asking a question is the best source of information, yet it is the least used.

## Bad news...

When I was with Scott Paper Company, I attended a seminar that wrapped-up with the CEO giving his views on a host of topics. He looked like the business leader from central casting with his air of confidence, excellent presentation and good looks. During the Q and A, I asked if he ever got mad.

He said we should have seen him after he was told that a new pulp mill was going to be $50 million over its $180 million budget. What angered him was not the overrun but that he was told too late to change the cost outcome. The overly confident engineers knew they were headed toward the overspending and they thought they could manage it through some unknown miracle and come within budget. His voice rose throughout his explanation but he concluded calmly that he had taken a vow never to shoot the messenger when he received bad news.

When giving bad news, the project team must initiate it early and not let a leak or audit expose it. A solution is not necessarily needed when you advise those up the line that there is a problem. As one engineer said, "You need to lay the pipe ahead of time so that when you need it, it works."

Remember, too, that there will be no incentive to give early warnings if the organization shoots the messenger, or handles the problem acceptably then bayonets the wounded after the battle is over.

# Bonuses...

During my career as a project manager, I found there was a wide range of attitudes about determining bonuses.

Receiving my first bonus in 1963 was the most instructive. In determining the amount, there was a complicated formula that measured annual performance against goals in areas of safety, cost, scrap, quality, volume targets and employee relations and a subjective rating given by my supervisor. At the time, my employer was so focused on scrap reduction that they multiplied by 2.7 the dollar value of the scrap generated to give it extra weight and force attention to it. The company said that the materials purchased and brought into the plant either went to the warehouse in the finished goods, down the sewer, up the stack or in the trash. Maximizing materials into finished goods obviously yielded the most profit.

The plant manager left a lasting memory with me when we met for the annual bonus award. He spoke my name, followed by, "Let's see, if you earned what you could have, you would be getting $2000." And with that, he slid banded stacks of $1 bills totaling $2000 out in the middle of his conference table. "But, no," he read from a list, "You only get $800." He moved $1200 off the table and handed me a check for the $800. The visual impact was not lost on me as in my next assignment I maxed out on the bonus by virtually eliminating the scrap.

With another employer, bonus opportunities were tied to one's ability to set and meet goals. When establishing a target it was important to know what yardsticks the senior managers used. One vice president, for example, ruled that if you overran the budget by one dollar, his evaluation of your cost performance was zero.

At the inception of a project with this company, I asked

the supervising vice president how he wanted targets set. He replied, "If my banker promises my loan on Wednesday and it is approved on Thursday, I am unhappy. However, if he says Friday and approval is on Thursday, I am a happy person. Please note the day of approval, Thursday, is the same in both examples." He knew the company culture was to reward favorable variances (actual results better than the target); hence, under-promise and over-perform was a project and personal axiom.

My idea for project bonuses parallels that of the World Series participants' payout. Without victory there are no fruits of success to share. Establish the measures of success at the beginning and designate a pot of money, say, 0.5% of the project's value. At the end of the project obtain a rating of the outcome and apply it as a percentage of the original pot. On a $20 million project the pot is $100,000. A final rating might be 85%, so $85,000 is available. The core project team votes shares to participants who had a significantly favorable impact on the project. It is essential to agree early on the core team. Agreeing to use this plan is a measure of trust and maturity, and a belief that bonus opportunities motivate people to produce positive results.

Some companies view bonuses as a substitute for good management and don't use them. Some use them as clubs. I recall one project team whose project had periodic ratings of the design consultants. At the first rating meeting, the project manager asked, "Should we rate them low to get their attention, or rate them high to keep them happy?" So much for objective scoring!

# Capital project systems...

Corporations have processes to identify, approve, fund and manage (via the project manager) capital investments. Some even evaluate the actual benefit resulting from the project. The processes vary, as does the compliance to the processes and their related procedures.

I worked in three different capital project cultures. The principal and universal lesson that I learned is that the specific outcomes that senior management desire must be understood and accepted early by those involved, otherwise the project is headed for failure.

One company focused on positive variances (actual results better than the target), safety performance, budget, schedule and startup quality and quantity. They didn't track eventual performance and profitability closely so they didn't lead their industry in return on assets. The firms that led in that area installed more frugal facilities that met but didn't needlessly exceed the target capacity.

Another insisted on first-rate equipment in the main process, few redundancies designed in, and removal of capacity bottlenecks after startup when it could be accomplished, based upon specific measured limitations.

The third, Procter & Gamble took a frugal approach after building a near-pharmaceutical quality toilet goods plant in Iowa City with stainless steel conveyors and glazed tile walls. Management decided that the next plant built would be a minimum-designed facility. So, their Sacramento synthetics plant was constructed at minimum cost. The unanticipated negative results were excessive downtime to repair things and limited access in the smaller building. No bypasses or redundancies were initially installed. The plant eventually had high reliability but it was an expensive effort to get there.

Whatever the "official" capital project system, the project team must comply with the management culture and their expectations if the project team is to be successful. Unfortunately, the management may focus on a fast startup that could result in higher capital and operating costs with reduced profitability.

# Changing horses midstream . . .

Making changes midway through a project can become a significant source of project problems and failures. In particular, changing project leadership during a project can be extremely detrimental.

In one instance, the accountable manager, who was the business vice-president, was changed in the middle of the project. The project's success factors and measurements were changed unilaterally. The product planned for the startup was altered.

Directives to the project manager put him at odds with the plant operations manager. They would meet for one hour each week to address issues but in practice this meeting was an hour-long fight. No one was happy and the outcome was not good. Production targets were not met and the list of post-startup problems grew by the day. An extended period of expensive remedies and hard work by new people finally got the facility operating acceptably.

My advice to a project manager whose project boss is replaced is to first negotiate the changes the new manager wants to make. Spend sufficient time to gain mutual understanding and acceptance of what will constitute project success. The time and energy spent in recalibrating expectations will be small in contrast with that spent in future confrontations, explanations and lengthy resolutions.

A professional project manager benefits from being flexible in some situations, but quiet acceptance of changing the bedrock parameters of an ongoing project is a guarantee of failure.

# Check those shovels . . .

As he walked into the construction trailer, my boss asked our field accountant for the contractor's latest time and material billing. Receiving it, he stepped to the contractor's trailer and told the site manager that he wanted to see the seven shovels that were a line item on the tool rental list. Three people searched for an hour and found only five of the seven. My boss then asked for an audit of the total invoice and privately advised our construction manager that if he ever found this situation again there would be one less construction manager on our payroll.

I also saw a few illegal activities and shady practices that can result from greed and non-existent, or ineffective, checks and balances. For example, one office manager put his personal car repairs on the contractor's monthly invoice to our company. The lesson learned? Audit the books routinely, especially on reimbursable work.

One situation that an audit wouldn't catch came to light two years after the event. A local wire and cable supplier told us that his firm had been approved to supply material after giving the major contractor's site superintendent a new pickup truck. Ethical pressure has reduced this behavior greatly during the past forty years, but it still exists, so ask questions.

I like the two guidelines: Don't steal it unless you can live off it for the rest of your life. And, if what you are doing was on the front page of tomorrow's paper, would you be comfortable with it?

## Cleverness...

Examples of clever solutions to problems are often found as anecdotes in magazines. But the one I admired most was from my own experience at a plant I worked in on Staten Island.

An employee was leaving the plant at the end of his shift. The gatehouse guard asked to look into the employee's lunch box. The employee refused. Following standard procedure, the guard took the employee's name and advised him to report to the plant manager's office the next day at 10 AM.

At the 10 AM meeting, the employee, accompanied by his shop steward, explained to the plant manager that he had refused to open his lunch box because there had been a parakeet inside. A fellow worker wanted to buy it but couldn't make up his mind so the employee was taking the parakeet back home. He thought that if he opened his lunchbox for the guard it might escape. The plant manager thought for a few moments then delivered his decision, "Two weeks off without pay for soliciting personal business on company property."

The manager was thinking creatively. Rather than get into an opening-or-not-opening the lunch box argument, he thought of an alternative solution. There is a benefit in taking the time to think about alternatives that will accomplish the right result. When you are in the middle of a project, the enemy is time. Take the time to think and don't try to resolve things too quickly.

On a project at a Weyerhaeuser mill, the mill manager came to me and asked why we weren't using Weyerhaeuser lumber in our construction. I offered that we were doing the work lump sum and a specification, not a specific manufacturer, governed the contractor. The mill manager said he was getting heat from the local union about not using our lumber and asked me to look into it. I asked the contractor to buy a unit load of 2x4s that was plainly labeled with the Weyerhaeuser logo and to place it in front of the new construction. That quieted the union, eased the mill manager's stress level and eventually provided some free lumber for the mill maintenance folks.

On a new Procter & Gamble cake mix plant, we expected some important visitors from Cincinnati just before startup. The day before the visitors arrived, the project manager had a local trucking company bring in three trailer rigs and load them with equipment and materials we didn't think we would need in the interim. The visitors were impressed with the neatness and austerity of the plant. The trucker returned the loads later and all was well.

## Common enemy...

Building an effective project team of diverse individuals, each of whom has their own agenda, can be a challenge for a number of reasons: business history says competition brings out the best in everyone; management wants to see the project team defending the company's interests vigorously; team members believe in the win-lose philosophy and their evaluations do not look good when their employer loses. This reflects the zero-sum game philosophy that says there is a total value in the project and the participants should maximize their shares.

On a $400 million project I managed, the contractor's site manager came to me after being on board for about six months. He observed that even though we all went through team-building exercises and were committed to a partnering agreement, his team exhibited a lack of cohesion that he had experienced on prior projects. When I asked why, he said the major difference was that in his previous experience, one member organization was the enemy of all the other groups. The presence of a common enemy united them regardless of their natural conflicts or "an enemy of my enemy is an ally."

On one project, his company was the enemy of the owner's team, the design engineer, the plant organization and the suppliers. He didn't like his role with no allies, but he said his team worked together well and his company made their target profit. "It wasn't fun and I didn't get invited back, but within my team we felt good about our performance and each of our roles in achieving it."

We did not elect a "black hat" on our project but his observation did underline the human desire to conquer something. The energy might be focussed on eliminating waste instead; such as, time, money, materials or ignorance.

You will, however, encounter those people on projects who glory in being the target of another's animosity. They feel that they (and hence, their employer) must be doing things right if their actions cause other folks in this zero-sum game to accuse them of doing something wrong.

## Confidence...

In my experience, the three principal assets that make individuals successful are competence, confidence and commitment. People generally agree on the competency requirements to do a job. Commitment to the task at hand is also fairly obvious. Confidence, however, is a subject for discussion since having too much appears as arrogance and having too little as the fear of doing anything.

The best lesson in what appropriate confidence means came during my initial two-week indoctrination into the Corps of Engineers at Fort Belvoir in 1958. We were a fresh group of newly minted second lieutenants commissioned out of college ROTC, except one. He was a first lieutenant in the Armored Corps who was changing branches.

Command assignments were rotated daily. The day the first lieutenant was company commander, he marched us to the parade ground. The assigned training officers, all formerly enlisted men who went through OCS, were professional harassers who had no love for commissioned college boys. There was a narrow bridge over a ditch adjacent to the parade ground. It took concentration to give the "column left" command on the correct foot and at the right time so that all four ranks of the column would march across the bridge. Too early or too late and one or more ranks would march through the muddy ditch. Two of the harassers were at work on the first lieutenant and, predictably, he missed the mark. Two ranks went on the bridge and two ranks waded through the ditch.

One of the training officers screamed, "Lieutenant, why did you march your men through that filthy, infested, stinking ditch?" In an equally loud voice, the first lieutenant at once responded, "Because that's where I wanted them to go!" The training officers were silent and went to other tasks; his confidence showed them who was in charge. The lesson was not lost on us.

Confident people know what they are doing, and they will deliver their services where needed, in the right way, at the right time and with good judgement. Management wants project managers with good judgement; good judgement comes from experience; experience comes from bad judgement. Nobody wants to pay for the consequences of bad judgement but it is part of the learning process for those who will learn.

Individuals on any project team need to have a high level of skill and judgement in both planning the work and then working the plan. Look for people who are competent, committed and confident. Trying to achieve outstanding results with average people not willing to learn is a crapshoot. Occasionally they will succeed, but not as a rule. The Harvard Business School turns out captains of industry, not only due to the excellent education, but because they only admit first-round draft choices. Golden geese come from golden eggs.

## Confidentiality...

When I was with Procter & Gamble, I discovered that it was a very private company. I thought that their level of privacy was a business norm. You never talked business with a non-P & G'er, and even with fellow employees there was a "need-to-know" expectation.

In the Ivorydale Technical Center in Cincinnati, the engineering drawings that were considered proprietary were printed on pink paper. We were subjected to security tours on random weekends to check for any pink paper left in the open on desks. If you were found to have any on your desk, you were warned with a discussion about the company's edge in technology and the need for secrecy. In the plants, there were specific pieces of commercial equipment that had been improved by P & G engineers for a unique function or to operate at a significantly higher rate. On the related drawings, there were large stamped messages to never allow the drawing to be seen by the manufacturer and to call a phone number in Cincinnati should you have an operational problem or question.

P & G's entry into the paper sector demonstrated how sharing information affected confidentiality in that industry. In the 50s, P & G said that expansion of existing businesses would not meet profit objectives so they went shopping. Their criteria for a product was a low-cost consumer disposable capable of being advertised on TV. They looked at over-the-counter drugs, paper towels, facial tissue and toilet tissue plus a few other segments.

When they looked more deeply into paper products, they discovered three things: there was no competition (Scott owned toilet tissue, Kimberly-Clark had Kleenex and paper towels were split up); the paper companies suffered from management and leadership styles out of the 1800s; and everyone knew what you couldn't do because the companies shared information openly through their professional societies. While working for Scott Paper Company and Weyerhaeuser Company in later years, I saw evidence of P & G's conclusions.

Secrecy and exclusivity are difficult to maintain in the project world. An attitude of independent professionalism together with the movement of project professionals among companies, suppliers, engineering consultants and construction contractors augers against it. I have heard this expressed as, "I'm a project manager; I do my job in the best manner I know; it just happens that the XYZ Company signs my check."

In a project, a company can gain an edge over a competitor without needing to resort to secrecy if it has the ability to do the right things very well. Vince Lombardi once said, "I'll give anybody Green Bay's play book because only I have the players who know how to execute." With similar education, professional societies and a shelf of project management books, the likelihood of any firm having the best procedures and techniques is small. The difference is in the quality of the execution.

# Constructability...

An early evaluation of the constructability of a design can save money and maybe some time. It is a good idea to have experienced, cost-conscious construction supervisors come to the design office early in the engineering phase to offer cost-saving construction ideas that can be included in the design. For example, the concrete foundations for a certain size-range of pumps were sized the same to minimize the concrete forms needed and to maximize reuse. At Procter & Gamble, the pumps were mounted on the legs of the tanks, where possible, to eliminate the concrete and save floor space.

Some constructability efforts have gone off track because the designers thought they were being second-guessed and resented it. They didn't accept that an intelligent dollar spent in the design could save five to ten times that in the field. In the extreme, some designs cannot be constructed. Additionally, if the project is tracking reworked drawings as a measure of design quality, the designer will not start until he has all the information thereby avoiding the risk of revising the drawing and being assessed for a "change."

Some design firms will try to avoid a constructability effort by hiding behind their concern about professional liability. An aside on the engineer's liability insurance: if the firm has $10 million in coverage, it applies on an annual basis so that if another company has a $9 million claim filed ahead of you, there is only $1 million left to cover your work in that year.

Constructability success relies on using experienced people and creating a team atmosphere where ideas are described, evaluated and utilized for the greatest benefit.

# Contingency...

Estimates require a contingency factor as an allowance for the unknown. There are a number of upper-level managers unfamiliar with capital projects that think this is a slush fund for changes over the life of the project. Contingency is a percentage of the total project cost that covers unknown but historically incurred costs that might result from chance events. Examples might include a strike in a supplier's shop that causes extra costs, bad weather delays beyond the norm or a tight labor market resulting in less than competitive bidding or higher labor costs.

In my experience, these unexpected costs get funded from wherever funds are available and accessible, and through means which least rock the project boat and upper management. The project manager and the decision-maker need to agree on how the contingencies, unlisted items and any other funds that are "allowances" are to be used. They must also agree on the approval process, with a bias toward lower dollar amounts to show management that changes are justified. This may not prevent a conflict later but it should minimize the number of those conflicts.

Conventional wisdom doesn't question inclusion of cost contingencies under the headings of construction contingency, unlisted items and escalation; but try to include a scheduling contingency to allow for some delays over the life of the project and you will meet with silence at best and verbal abuse at worst.

# Cost management...

With the four corporations I've worked for, I have seen two approaches to project capital cost management.

In one style, the cost is set at appropriation and becomes a benchmark that governs all behavior. The first step is to get approval of an upper-end-of-the-estimate figure to comply with the under-promise and over-perform culture, if present. These companies work on variances. Promise $1 million and have a cost underrun, the project is heroic with awards for all. But overrun the costs by the same amount and no one wins. There is much more time and energy devoted to keeping the actual result favorable to the target than is initially spent determining if the $1 million is correct in the first place.

Procter & Gamble practiced an alternate approach. People were educated to have a cost-saving attitude. All costs, regardless of source or historical expenditure, were questioned with, "Is there any reason this item of cost can't be eliminated?" This process was periodically applied to initially-included items as well as the evolving project's detailed scope items. This frugal approach, which has a mixed reputation in the project world, is given names like "the elimination approach" or "value engineering." There is a useful observation made by the money-saving, value thinker: "Whether my glass is half-full or half-empty, my glass is too big!"

# Delegation...

There is something about the behavior of most engineers that tends to make them control disciples. It may come from the fact that in engineering education there are only correct or incorrect answers, or it may be the rigidity of the lines on the paper or the computer screen. The adage, "If you want it done right, do it yourself," is often heard. The downside is that one person can't do it all. There are alternative ways of doing things and the outcome is what is most important.

Early in my career I was supervising a contractor who had to change a main steam valve at 3:00 AM. I was there in plenty of time and things were going well. At 2:40 AM my boss arrived. He didn't say too much, just watched. Later in the day I asked him why he had shown up the night before. He finally said he was worried that if anything had gone wrong, he would have had to step in. I told him if he didn't trust me to do the work delegated to me, I could easily get into the "why worry" mode. If it goes wrong, the boss will fix it! Instead, he could have reviewed with me earlier in the day any possible problems, gauged what my responses were and provided suggestions.

Each manager has a different comfort level with delegation, both in what they expect from above and what they grant to subordinates. There is no right answer except to do what experience and judgment say is best. By delegating, I promoted responsibility and built confidence and skill in those who worked for me.

# Design documents...

A construction contractor requires just the right number of documents to build the intended facility. If there are too few documents there will be pricey change orders and delays; if too many, the engineering costs will be excessive and the contractor's expertise may be under-utilized.

A design-build arrangement, where the design engineer and contractor join as one entity, is thought to be a good way to get the right balance. A variation adds the major equipment supplier to the partnership and provides one-stop shopping as well as a focus of guarantees. I have been project manager of several of these combinations and have observed a few others. The lessons are many.

On one project, the design engineer had never done any lump-sum engineering nor been led by a construction contractor who was the primary. The engineer wanted to supply drawings that covered everything. The contractor wanted only what drawings were minimally necessary for construction, thereby holding down the design costs. Since the design engineer had a lump-sum contract with the contractor, the project was completed with some difficulty, especially the schedule. There was the "original" schedule, followed by the "recovery" schedule, after which came the "optimum" schedule.

While waiting for the airplane after the dedication ceremony for this project, I remember the design firm's manager saying, "I learned a lot on this project, but I never want to be involved in another one like it." For the project manager, the lesson is this: use experienced companies and individuals that have had success working on your type of contract arrangement. Otherwise, you are going to absorb the cost of their education, which is unknown until the end.

# Diversity...

We hire those who look most like us.

In the 1950s, the plant manager of a Procter & Gamble facility said that in his opinion, money spent on recruiting was largely wasted because the people hired were the ones most like us -- education, ethnicity, social status. He felt we only needed to go on campus, do a quick and primarily visual interview of those with degrees the company desired, and offer jobs to the people who we were comfortable with and who resembled us most. He even had data to prove his point.

The normal recruiting procedure was to have a student sign-up sheet posted on campus in the spring. When we visited the school, we conducted a 30-minute interview with each student and made a first cut. Those who were not a good fit were sent a letter wishing them good fortune. The others were invited to the facility for a later visit.

The invitees spent a day at our plant getting to know us and the operation and undergoing three additional interviews. A member of plant management was assigned to meet the student in the morning to assure the day's schedule was met. A successful interview resulted in a written offer. At 8:00 AM, this particular plant manager saw the visitor first and then had his secretary (within 20 seconds of seeing the student) make a determination of whether an offer would be made or not. She correctly predicted 24 of 25 outcomes. P & G did not change their recruiting procedure and you may wonder how this iconoclastic plant manager survived his recruiting process recommendation.

We become comfortable with those who don't bring much change into our life. In the past thirty years, we have slowly brought women and various ethnic groups into our project world for the variety and new perspectives they have to offer, and sometimes to meet legal requirements. However, attend the conventions involving the major contractors and look for women and minorities. Few are seen. Much remains to be done and it starts with encouraging a more diverse group of people to acquire degrees in technical fields.

# Education and training...

The effectiveness of an employer's efforts at improving the performance of project team members through education follows the standard distribution of the bell curve, slightly above the historic level of results. There are many factors contributing to the failure of education programs, such as: using a training assignment as a perk; skimping on the cost of training; failing to tie an employee's pay to performance improvement; and ignoring in-house resources to do the training. The person who is the teacher learns the most, so with few exceptions, in-house project people should be the instructors. An education professional's input is needed in the mix to provide quality control for the effort. I spent a lot of time being trained and training others. The 80/20 rule applies — 20% of the training yields 80% of the benefit.

Education via the Internet can be effective for learning principles and procedures. The development of material for programmed learning is also worthwhile, as getting agreement on content will crystallize how a company thinks it should be doing projects.

Some subjects require person-to-person training such as in the practical application of making presentations, negotiating, interviewing and other areas where personal dynamics influence the outcome. Case studies and in-basket exercises are effective as they provide the best vehicle for learning in a realistic setting. A subject that should be taught is how things really get done in an organization.

Effective training requires the student to ask, "What's in it for me?" and should be answered positively by management if the student is going to be motivated to learn. One organization that I was part of looked at the training budget as a measure of how they were doing competitively against industry norms, rather than as the fuel for specific improvement of their own employees' performances.

Mentoring by a more experienced or knowledgeable employee is a beneficial training technique. This can work parallel with other training activities. I recall that Procter & Gamble had several key middle managers that would have high-potential individuals assigned to them for a year to learn their area of recognized expertise.

In my first job for Procter & Gamble, I was hired as a responsible manager and was not required to participate in a mind-numbing in-house training program. We learn the best by doing. As a previous co-worker of mine said, "It costs money to go to school."

Professional societies have only one value-added justification and that is transfer of knowledge. The newer societies are better at it, as their conferences focus on the aptness and quality of the content and presentation. The older organizations worry about anti-trust behavior and pay little attention to the usefulness of their activities. In some cases, being independent of these organizations pays off. When Procter & Gamble entered the paper industry in the late 1950s, they were not part of the established pulp and paper professional groups so their research was unencumbered by the shared knowledge of what wouldn't work.

# A few words...

A few words said at a critical moment can reveal a person's character and often will establish that person's reputation among his co-workers.

The manager of a large company's engineering division and I were discussing some matters at his desk. His assistant interrupted saying the construction manager at one of the plants was on the phone with an urgent call. I only heard one side of the call and it went, "Hi, Cliff...Was anyone hurt?... Call when you know more."

The engineering manager explained to me that the plant production crews were starting to occupy an almost completed warehouse when a forklift truck ran into an interior column causing four bays of the roof to collapse. Cliff was giving him an early warning so he would not be surprised and could respond to any other calls. He also didn't want to take up Cliff's time, as he knew it was a crisis situation. (Fortunately, no one was hurt.) This speaks to a lot of trust.

As a postscript, the contractor who was repairing the warehouse roof had stored materials on the adjacent roof bays. It rained heavily before he could do his work and water pooled under the materials causing two more bays to collapse. (Again, no one was injured.) If there is a lesson from this subsequent failure, it is that the most recent event (a column knocked out) probably received serious attention but other potential hazards were skimmed over. I once had a boss, who said, "Paul, no matter how well you think things are going, there is a land mine just waiting to be stepped on."

In an entirely different situation, I was in a plant manager's office of one of the company's midwestern plants. His wife walked in the door looking disheveled and said, "We've just been in an accident." The plant manager responded with, "How bad is the car damaged?" His distraught wife replied, "Don't you care anything about your children?" The plant manager followed her out, turning red with embarrassment as he realized what he had said.

Those swift, reactive responses reveal our beliefs and attitudes. Once said, those few words can never be unsaid. They mark you for life.

## Frankness...

Early in my career, two experiences impressed upon me the need for being frank with people.

I was a production department manager when a new foreman transferred into my unit. My group manager told me the new employee had been a marginal performer in the past and this assignment was a "last chance" for him. On his first day in the department, I scheduled a meeting with him and we talked about mutual expectations and other subjects. I got around to the "last chance" aspect of the assignment. He looked at me in a puzzled way and asked what I was talking about. He said that he saw this job as a chance to display his good work. I said we needed to talk more after I got some additional information.

I discussed the meeting with my group manager. He said that he would do some digging. What emerged was that the foreman's prior manager had given him a low evaluation but had never discussed it with him, hoping to avoid a difficult discussion. The plant manager demoted the prior manager. The foreman's record was cleaned up and he went on to perform as a good shift supervisor. Obviously, several people were educated, each with different tuition costs.

A later experience came as a result of an intense one-week training session on expanding skills in both interpersonal and push-for-production areas. Conventional wisdom has it that these two areas are mutually exclusive and as you ramp up on one you descend down the other. There was a self-evaluation exercise followed by a peer review that revealed the gaps between your view of yourself and others' view of you.

One fellow, after we shared our criticisms of him, went off into his own world lecturing us that we were wrong about him. Historically, he said his evaluations had been completely different from what we perceived. After some more of this monologue, someone asked, "If you are so good, why are you still a staff engineer after twenty years?" The man fell into his chair and in a soft voice accused his prior supervisors of not pressing him to improve his shortfall areas. The "white-washed" evaluations had made him feel good and he always got the average salary increase. He never did get around to telling us what he could have done to correct his rose-colored view of himself.

Giving a frank evaluation is a learned skill. It can be difficult to do, but it is necessary for personal development and the consequences of not doing it are great. Your employees don't want to wake up one day to the fact that they have wasted years of their lives.

# Goal setting...

Every project has goals set for it. They may be called key performance factors, outcomes, standards of performance or whatever management uses as a current yardstick. They include safety, cost, schedule, quality, unplanned production interruptions, customer satisfaction plus whatever else makes sense for the particular project. Much is written on the subject and there are a variety of systems in use. One, which makes sense to me but is rarely discussed, is the actual return achieved by the end product. That measure can shed light on the quality of the original management decision to invest.

There are other goals that should also be included but are usually not written down. They are the expectations of behavior between the project manager's boss and the project manager. Specifically, I always asked my project boss what three things, if I did them, would really upset him. The range of answers included: "Don't surprise me. Tell me before you tell anyone at the home office. Don't issue any orders to my people. Make sure the construction site is kept clean. Don't make any separate deals that I don't approve." This beneficial discussion got these subjects on the table before there was a problem.

I would then volunteer to my boss that I had three things that if he did them, I would be upset. I tailored these to my current knowledge of the specifics. They included: "If you have a problem with me or my team tell me first. Don't exclusively rely on your other managers for information. Don't hide your biases; if you want something, say so ahead of time." I also asked him to treat the project people the same as his plant folks and not to change any project goals without a discussion.

It helps to know the boss's opinion of project managers and project work. One plant manager said he would consider my behavior positive if he got late-night calls from the local police asking his help in getting his operations manager and me to stop buying drinks for each other. We didn't meet that expectation but got his point.

An additional fruitful discussion should bring into the open what risks the boss is willing to take and how he wants to participate. Again these discussions help lay the foundation for the temporary but hopefully productive relationship.

A Weyerhaeuser vice-president once told me that he tried to make goal setting more realistic and to modify the reward system to better reward good results and not reward negative outcomes. However, he said he felt as if he were bowling with a curtain between him and the pins. He didn't know if he was getting strikes, spares or gutter balls. The corporation was not ready for that change.

A last comment on goals: The ultimate measure of success is did they invite you back?

# History...

Keeping an accurate and useful history of significant project data is a subject that is greatly ignored in the engineering and construction industry. I am not talking about the routine estimating data like work-hours/foot of six-inch stainless steel pipe or the average percentage use of contingency.

A design consultant illustrated what I am talking about as we were starting a $25 million project at a western plant. He said that he maintained records that sorted projects by company and location. His firm had done over 50 projects for this particular plant, and the data showed that the actual engineering design work-hours at startup averaged 140% of the work-hours estimated at the time the design contract was approved. He had back-up information that gave the source of the extra hours: changes, slow delivery of supplier information, incorrect historic drawings of the plant and other causes. His point in displaying this was to influence our expectations and not have us forecast a low number based on high hopes.

I thought this was the kind of information our company should maintain but there was no appetite for it. Senior managers felt that if we based predictions on past history, we would not improve. Perhaps, but can't we at least use history as a starting point for measurement of progress?

# Hoopla...

Generating publicity for a project with buttons, hardhat stickers, banners, souvenirs, lunches and whatever else, draws attention to the project and its successful execution. The objective is to build a sense of pride among those working on the project.

This also has a downside. Competition causes some to want to outdo their peers. This is especially true of consultants who use this as a means of advertising. There isn't much originality in the same old belt buckles, jackets and ball hats that are favorites with many groups. Suspenders with company logos are a welcome change. I challenge you to come up with more creative hoopla that more closely focuses on common objectives, project outcomes and the daily work.

You can also get into the controversial area of bonuses and incentives. Some company cultures welcome this; others see it as a waste of money and a substitute for good managing. And there can be a downside to bonuses. The recipient may feel entitled to the maximum, but when it is not awarded, feels as though he has lost something instead of achieving something. Whatever you choose to do, some people will be unhappy. The amount and quality of the award or the recipient chosen will raise somebody's ire.

There are also conflicts between plant people and project people. In one case, at the end-of-project drawing for a major prize to celebrate the project's safety record, the plant operations and maintenance union members were deemed ineligible for the prize. Fortunately, a contractor's employee won making the potential conflict moot, but it illustrates the point.

## Issue and conflict resolution...

At the beginning of a project there is a "feel good" period, a kind of honeymoon, where success appears assured and all will be sweetness and light. At this stage, you are reluctant to develop a conflict resolution procedure because you don't want to deal with negative issues. However, develop your resolution process early and do not wait until you are in the middle of a fight.

Projects normally have issues and conflicts. If you don't resolve them promptly, they grow in megatonnage and become more toxic. I have heard project teams say they don't have enough time to resolve an issue when it comes up and that they will do it at the end of the project. That approach yields dissatisfaction, hard feelings and higher costs.

I have seen several good methods for resolving conflicts. One way is to agree on who the decision-maker will be and then have each party argue the other side's case. This doesn't change the facts but it assures that each side understands the other's point of view. This process allows resolution between the parties, usually without going before the decision-maker. History teaches that we don't listen. This assures listening. Also, if you take too many decisions to your supervisor, your ability to get things done will be questioned.

My favorite process divides all the project participants into several tiers of responsibility. At the lowest level, you have two days to resolve the issue. If it isn't resolved, it moves up the line for a five-day time limit. Next, it goes to the site managers for each of the parties for a seven-day maximum. Beyond that, it moves to the vice-presidents. This process keeps disagreements from lingering on and becoming more detrimental to relationships and to project outcomes. This works well since those with the most knowledge of the issue deal with it first. In order to be successful, this approach requires a level of trust among the participants.

Usually a project has an issue resolution process written into the contract. Scott Paper Company wanted every possibility covered in a contract and always in Scott's favor. On one project, the work was 50% complete and we still did not have a signed contract with the construction company. In frustration we finally agreed that the remedies available to each party were those determined by common law. I might add that Scott assigned newly hired in-house lawyers to write construction contracts. Draw your own conclusions.

On a major Weyerhaeuser project, the contractor and Weyerhaeuser's project management agreed to accumulate all changes and settle at the end. The contractor's number was $7 million and Weyerhaeuser's was $500,000. The contractor threatened legal action but later settled for $1 million. Who fared best? No one knows. The contractor was never on Weyerhaeuser's bidders list again.

## Key numbers...

Anticipating real problems before they become showstoppers is a beneficial skill in managing a project. Key numbers can be a good benchmark. Experience and intuition help but there is no substitute for simple bits of data to send warning signals.

In the 1970s, I met the person who managed the construction of the Boeing 747 assembly building in Everett, Washington. It's the largest volume building in the world. I asked him how he got his head around managing such a large project. He said Boeing utilized computer-generated schedule status reports, but by the time you read, analyzed, then decided how to deal with any problems, the construction had moved on to new work.

Instead, before construction of the building began, he calculated that the contractor, who was building the structure from rolling scaffolding, would have to move about 50 feet per day. During the work he marked the floor every morning at 8 AM. If 50 or more feet of progress were made from yesterday's mark, he was amiable and easy to deal with. If the measurement were less than 50 feet, he would raise Cain.

This oversimplified example is useful to dispute the myth that with greater computer technology there is greater truth in the printout. The best scheduler I know did not use any sophisticated scheduling program. He talked to people and was always asking questions. His network schedules were simply displayed on drawing, not computer, paper. Thinking takes precedence.

There are other examples of using key numbers. One machine shop owner looks at the pounds of gears shipped each day — 500+ is good and 500- is an early warning of falling sales or backup in the shop. A restaurant owner checks on the number of guests waiting to be seated at 7:30 PM — 6+ is good and 6- is an indication that business is falling off.

Some history of what constitutes valid numbers is necessary to develop the warning limits. On a project it may be daily tons of steel placed, cubic yards of concrete poured or lineal feet welded. Use a quickly available item that is reliable and not subject to argument.

## Learning never ends...

The lessons that you personally learn carry the most weight in all your future work. Two of my most important first lessons were: (1) there was a lot I didn't know and (2) there were people who knew how to leverage simple bits of information effectively.

During my second day as a project engineer at a Duncan Hines cake mix plant on Staten Island, I overheard a conversation between Procter & Gamble's instrumentation engineer and the contractor's pipefitter foreman. The foreman said there wasn't enough clearance to install a large control valve with the stem vertical as shown on the drawings. The engineer asked the body color of the valve. Green was the answer. The engineer then said the valve stem could be in any direction, even upside down. The foreman thanked the engineer and left. This conversation bewildered me so I asked the engineer about what I had just heard. He replied, "Each control valve supplier uses a different color. Green means a Fisher Porter valve and it can be installed with the stem in any orientation."

The lesson was simple and universal; you can always learn and the lessons can come from anyone. A shortcoming of some college graduates is their belief that when they get their degree their education is complete.

Another example is a classic engineering case study of a bridge failure during construction in Australia. It was called the Westgate Bridge and had an innovative box girder design. There were several parties involved: the local governmental bridge authority, the construction contractor, the site supervisors, the labor union and the design firm based in England. The study was a very thorough one with many arrows in the body of the project. The greatest lesson for me, beyond witnessing the lack of communication among groups with dueling agendas, was recognizing that the bridge authority manager only tried to prevent the mistakes he had been involved with in past projects. He rarely sought out new issues as he felt his learning was complete. A second important message from this case study was: "When you are in trouble, you are alone and when you are alone, you are in trouble." The obvious point is to use your internalized lessons only as a starting checklist.

Some Chevron engineers once told me that even though they had some good lessons in their database, when a new project came along they would convene the new team with people who had worked on the most recent similar installation. This closed-door session was invaluable, as it was unfiltered personal experience. The new team applied their knowledge and judgment to the information and planned accordingly. Project results improved.

## Loyalty and trust...

While I was working on a project for Scott Paper Company in Everett, Washington, I sat next to a business vice-president for the company on a flight from Seattle to Philadelphia. He expressed his views to me on what he saw as a lack of loyalty by project engineers.

According to him, senior management often felt that project engineers didn't share the company's agenda for making money. In his opinion, the project people, suppliers, contractors and design consultants all belonged to the same technical fraternity that neglected to hold each other's feet to the fire on decisions tied to making money for the company. He gave process control as an example. Sophisticated systems were installed; then, after two years, were mostly disconnected or bypassed. He offered that in some applications, a bucket and a stopwatch would have been sufficient.

I tried to mount rebuttals to his points, but some of them were valid. In my experience, over-designing by engineers comes from wanting the latest in technology but should be questioned more thoroughly by the decision-makers in management. It is also true that many engineers look at themselves as independent technical professionals with their employer just happening to be the name on their paycheck. Besides, loyalty isn't what it used to be. Scott Paper Company's later experience at the hands of Al Dunlap, who sold the company to Kimberly Clark, proved this point.

Once, at a construction seminar, I heard a Seattle commercial developer deliver the same message as the Scott vice-president. He felt that the engineers, designers, suppliers and contractors in the industrial arena did not question thoroughly enough the justification for all cost components. He estimated that up to 20% of industrial investment was in extra, unproductive assets.

When I look back at Procter & Gamble in this context, I see that they addressed the issue by assigning people during their career to jobs both inside and outside of engineering so there would be a universal understanding of project work. They also taught in all their activities the importance of thrift in making money.

In a project setting, it is important to recognize that there are often issues around loyalty and trust because relationships are temporary. It is important to know the environment you are operating in and not be surprised when engineers, designers, etc. do not share the same objectives as management. Observe, ask questions of those with more experience and make it your responsibility to be trusted to meet your company's goals.

## Mutual objectives...

A project is both temporary and complex. Temporary, in that it exists for a short period of time in terms of a company's lifetime or a participant's career. Complex because it consists of full-time people who work for different companies, part-time contributors and arms-length stakeholders who may have little influence but are affected significantly by the outcome. Obviously each of the people or groups will have some agenda conflicts but they will also have some mutual objectives.

A Procter & Gamble vice-president once asked me, "What does P & G make?" "Soap, synthetic detergent, toothpaste, shortening," I replied. "Wrong," he said. "P & G makes money. We know something about the manufacturing and merchandising of the products you mention, but we make money. If housewives started beating clothes on rocks by the stream then we would build a rock factory." The successful project manager should understand money and profit because each company involved in the project will have the mutual objective of being profitable.

Jack Creighton, a past Weyerhaeuser CEO, talked about shared purpose and mutual objectives using the example of the "black canoe" that comes from the traditional lore of a Northwest Coast tribe, the Haida. The story tells of a diverse set of paddlers in the black canoe who must work together to reach a common destination if they are to survive. Our project group used the example of the canoe as we encountered problems, recognizing that we shared the same goals and needed to act in concert toward a mutually understood and accepted set of success factors. Conflict was expected and used constructively. The concept of the canoe was easily understood and hard to argue against.

Having believed for years that competition brings out the

best in everyone, I have trouble falling in love with partnering, preferred suppliers and the general trend toward exclusiveness in the supply chain. I know some firms have done it well and have benefited their bottom line. What I have experienced with the modern partnership culture is a subordination of profits and value to the testimonials favoring our "wonderful working relationship."

The growing industry of team-building and partnering facilitation has been increasingly popular in recent years. External facilitators periodically meet with the team and focus on getting everyone working on the same page. There are some excellent folks doing this work but don't expect miracles. Project participants, with their varieties of reward systems, beliefs and behaviors, are hesitant to commit to common objectives, as they want to avoid the fallout of someone else's failure. This doesn't surface unless there is a crisis that tests them.

I believe the greatest value of team-building activities lies in the open discussions about understanding another's point of view, culture or observed behavior rather than in the documents that come from the sessions.

# Negotiating...

Skillful negotiating is an essential requirement for anyone who wants to achieve a higher level of responsibility in the project business. There are hundreds of situations that occur during a project that demand negotiation, be it a brief conversation or the extended formality of a serious legal settlement.

Win-win is the preferred outcome but often not all parties will agree. Many believe in a zero-sum game — what one side loses, the other side wins. Regardless of one's persuasion there is a key point to recognize: to be successful, negotiators must like to negotiate. The techniques of good negotiating can be taught but what makes negotiators effective is their comfort in negotiating. They enjoy it!

On one of my projects, we were having issues with a supplier who was taking advantage of us from both a cost and schedule standpoint, and was not meeting the requirements of the contract. Our manager for that area had difficulty being firm with the supplier's representative. The usual sequence of events when a problem arose included the arrival of the supplier's home office representative, a meeting between him and our manager, followed by a change order favoring the supplier's position. Digging into this revealed that our manager had no stomach for conflict and wouldn't press our interests against the "struggling" supplier. Even though this manager had learned negotiating skills in professionally taught seminars, he disliked the process and therefore was ineffective. Once this shortcoming surfaced, the project purchasing manager successfully led the negotiations.

Another aspect of the importance of good negotiating is that it be proportional to the amount of money at risk. We might spend hours defining the engineering details of a $50,000 item yet not be willing to spend the same time and talent to negotiate a $100,000 outcome.

When bad weather interfered with his productivity, one contractor asked for additional money beyond his estimated weather allowance in his bid on a lump sum job. In our negotiations, rather than saying "no," I offered to reimburse him once he established a pattern of returning his unspent weather allowances when the weather was more favorable to the project.

You are the steward of your company's assets and reputation. Insist on what the contract promises to deliver. Understand that good negotiators like to negotiate. Assigning negotiations to someone who hasn't the desire is like teaching a pig to sing. You don't like the song and it irritates the pig.

# Open listening...

You can learn something from anyone if you spend the time to develop the trust necessary for the transfer of ideas. You must also open your listening and then use what you have learned.

I once worked with another project manager, Phil, who was a source of some excellent listening techniques that served me well. He and I were project managers on adjacent areas of a new pulp and paper mill in Mississippi. One firm was doing the engineering and construction, so he and I spent a good deal of time together.

One afternoon, several process control engineers and the technical representative for the equipment supplier were reviewing the architecture and operation of the process control system that would be installed in both our areas. The presentation got progressively more complicated and people were interrupting to add information or to disagree. I was becoming confused and I knew Phil was too. He said, "Let's stop a minute. I would like the supplier's rep to diagram, in simple terms, how the system will work." The rep started but it soon became apparent that he couldn't do it. "Why don't we break and reconvene when the diagram can be drawn," I said. It was two weeks until we met again. Phil told me that he always found it effective to ask for a diagram or flow chart to explain something complicated he didn't understand, or if he suspected he was being given a "snow job."

In the course of that project, we also made monthly presentations to senior management. Phil was unhappy with his presentation skills, so he asked me if I would critique his work and he would do the same for me. "You bet," was my reply, as I appreciated his help.

## Personal targets...

Several years ago at a contractors conference, I heard an 80-year-old contractor speak about his guiding principle for success in business.

He and a teen-aged friend were working at the Anaconda smelter in Montana in the late 1930s. They were unhappy with working for wages and decided to become a two-man construction company. After exploring work opportunities in the surrounding area, they thought the best bet was laying pipe for sewer and water lines. After they quit the smelter, they started their first job laying a water line for the county.

Upon arriving at the site with the material and equipment, they pounded a stake into the ground where they thought they would finish working at day's end. They reached the stake at sundown. When the job was completed, they figured their costs against what the county's contract paid. The profit was exactly what he and his friend would have netted at the smelter. The lesson he took away that made his company successful for 60+ years was: "Always set your stake out a little farther."

# Planning...

The necessity for project planning is a given. It begins with viewing major areas of the project as though you had a 30,000-foot vantage point and then establishing key milestone dates. But it has amazed me over the years how two problem situations can evolve related to planning, or I should say, non-planning. The first is that someone else is responsible for the planning. The second is that the various interest groups involved want to begin by planning the details. With their competing agendas, they are eager to establish their positions quickly and gain an edge for themselves. They support the notion that whoever gets there first has the advantage.

Planning is not fun like moving dirt and pouring concrete. Some stakeholders (anyone whose future may be affected by the outcome of the project) believe that if they provide for their own requirements first, they have done their planning. They don't have an appreciation for the interplay of all the requirements and how some are mutually exclusive. There is no question that it is the project manager's task to sort this out. A most useful tool is to conduct a short project management school that involves the identified stakeholder representatives.

A project manager I know once said that planning would happen, hopefully early and intelligently, as in "plan the work, then work the plan." The last place planning should occur is at the end of a shovel but I've seen it happen that way.

The key tool in planning is the overall schedule. One of my best project experiences was on a developmental technology project. During feasibility we met with the participants and stakeholders to list all the required activities we collectively could think of. It wasn't perfect but it worked. We then sequenced the activities and estimated durations. Each player wanted to get into the details of their specialty and didn't want to think about interfaces and consequences, so scheduling required a joint effort until everyone involved understood and accepted the results. This critical path exercise became the planning document that was subsequently spot-welded and wire-brushed with corrections as the project progressed. It was credited with being the key document in the project.

## Plant staff on projects...

Using input from plant operations and maintenance personnel is a feature of project management that has a wide range in practice.

Some companies use very little input from plant personnel. The engineers design and install what is required and commercially available. From the company's point of view, plant folks want extras and gold plating because they know that what is not included with the initial facility will be difficult to justify later.

Other companies believe that involving plant personnel in the project generates a sense of ownership of the new facility. These projects often have quick startups. But there can be a downside. Plant staff will want to include all the expensive bells and whistles. Because ongoing plant operations are focussed on successfully "getting the wash out" every day, the best plant personnel are kept on the existing production and maintenance jobs. The available people who are not needed to get the wash out are assigned to the project; in other words, second-tier employees.

Also, I rarely found a plant operations manager who understood that committing his best people to the project was only a risk to productivity in the short-term. In addition, some key plant people are reluctant to work on a project because they find it risky to leave a position where they are "king" to join a diverse group where the outcome is unknown.

New plants in new locations can generally get good operations people for the startup. However, good startup managers are not always good steady-state operators.

Most companies I worked for did not exercise the same rigor when evaluating capital dollars as they did when looking at operating and maintenance costs. A slow startup occurs with the frugal approach but the overall value to the company is usually greater. The hard fact is that the companies with little plant staff input have better financial returns.

## Procurement...

Companies have purchasing or procurement departments to buy goods and services. A capital project requires a significant purchasing effort. All the money spent for engineering design, equipment, construction and materials, less the salaries and expenses of the owner's project team, flows through purchase orders.

The lessons I learned in this purchasing arena are many. The primary one is have an experienced purchasing professional devoted 100% to the project effort. Smaller projects, especially, will use part-time or shared people and the skill, dedication and follow-up are not there. It is also possible to make the error of believing that any purchasing professional can accomplish project purchasing. Not true.

I once saw a sign in the kitchen of a fast-food restaurant that read, "If we buy it by the pound, weigh it; if by count, count it; and does the quality match our specification?" The same applies to projects.

Another lesson I learned is never to ask a supplier, engineer or contractor to do something outside his experience. You will probably pay twice as much for the result as you expect.

On one project, we bought motors from the supplier and shipped them to the pump manufacturer's shop to have them mounted and balanced. They were then shipped to the job site where they had to be re-balanced in the field. We subsequently discovered that the pump manufacturer routinely bought more motors than we did. If they had furnished them, the motors would have been less expensive and shop balancing would have been at no charge.

On a different project we had an offshore supplier provide operator training documents and classroom training.

They had never done this in the United States before and didn't realize they couldn't fulfill our requirements. It was a failure. We ended up hiring a local training consultant to sort out and accomplish the training.

## Project justification...

Early on, a project will require a preliminary financial analysis that displays its rate of return, net present value and whatever other financial measures are required by those who approve projects. This is straightforward in theory. My experience is that the analysis can be biased when the project sponsor wants the project approved. He may influence the data, lower the capital costs, raise the revenue value, shorten the schedule or lower the operating costs.

In one instance, a business vice-president read in an industry journal that a competitor had built a new paper machine for $39 million. He did some preliminary calculations that indicated a similar installation at one of our plants would yield a 30% return on the investment. He initiated an in-house engineering study.

In an early step in the project definition process, the project engineer sat with the vice-president and his manufacturing manager to flesh out some details. It turned out that the mill location for the new machine had no excess steam or electrical capacity. As a result, the preliminary estimate came to $48 million and the justification disappeared. The vice-president was irate and not at all happy with the result or with our engineering group, but stopping the project was the best choice for the company.

On one $25 million project, I recall sitting with the president, business vice-president and mill manager going over the project details prior to a meeting of the board of directors. The president asked the mill manager how he felt about the project. He replied that he could understand the equipment needs, the schedule, the capital cost estimate and the impact on his mill, but to him the revenue side was pure speculation. He had to take the future selling price per ton strictly on faith.

The business vice-president ran through his forecast, which satisfied the president, but not the mill manager. The project was approved nonetheless and away we went.

Some companies keep books on the outcome of capital investments to see how accurately the actual results meet the promises. Project sponsors develop a track record, and capital flows to those who get the most profitable results, and not necessarily to those who are the loudest or most influential and do not achieve promised returns. Business investment people are optimists who promise how wonderful it will be tomorrow, but it's often the tomorrow that never comes. A project manager needs to address those non-engineering factors that significantly affect the outcomes and expectations that surround a project.

## Project names...

Normally a project is given a unique name that serves as a label by which everyone recognizes the project quickly. It is also the name that appears on any publicity such as safety promotions, awards and most other documentation about the project. Confidential projects may have bland tags like T-25, XR7 and so on. Some get aggressive names using acronyms like Synthetic Test Installation-Natural Gas or STING.

If you put an undesirable label on your project, it will stick and may create a negative impression that won't help the project's image. I had a project in the mid-1980s that provided for separate pulping of several wood species. Its descriptive name was Fiber Optimization Project or FOP. Needless to say, the image of a fashion-conscious dandy never created any positive impressions.

If you have a choice, choose an upbeat, or at best, neutral project name.

## Promotions...

The lessons concerning promotions are well-documented in the literature. In my experience with four different companies, promotions usually went to the most deserving and methods of promotion reflected each company's culture.

In one case, employees were promoted from hourly or technician status to a supervisory role as a reward for good work. The system didn't provide for other kinds of rewards so promotion was the only choice. Often, the outcome was the creation of an unqualified supervisor and the corresponding loss of the excellent work the employee had been doing in his prior job.

At another company, an individual's increasing visibility in the organization became the evaluation criteria for promotion. Those who aspired to being promoted increased their chances by always keeping themselves on upper management's radar screen. However, even in that climate, most promotions were deserved.

"Followership" as a dimension of performance evaluation is often overlooked. When making an evaluation, I seldom saw subordinates asked for their views of their boss's leadership skills. Management relied on their own observations to evaluate candidates.

Another system for creating promotions involved a mentor in a high level job looking after the fortunes of a protégé at a lower level. At one time the New York City police department promoted almost exclusively those who had a "rabbi" in the senior leadership of the department. As one of my employers once said, you needed "queen bee jelly" on you to be on the fast track.

An important managerial trait is the ability to develop those who work for you and a measure of your performance is how many of your reports are promoted. This subject only gets attention when upper management is pursuing a wave of succession planning every two to three years.

Sometimes I saw that a manager's ability to develop people for promotion was not highly valued. If anything, managers held on to good people whose departure would make the manager's job more difficult. There was an attitude of not letting one's good people move up elsewhere in the company because it would be a loss to their current organization.

A rule at P & G was that a peer could not be promoted within a department. You couldn't take one of the guys and make him the boss. Not a bad rule.

The lesson for the project manager with regard to promotions is if you have someone you feel is worthy of moving up, you need to press your advocacy. Otherwise, since a project's life is short, a good person may continue to be assigned the same tasks on subsequent projects.

# Providing help...

At some point, every project professional will be sent out to help rescue another project that is in trouble. How you deal with this will influence your reputation. Even well-run projects have problems and if you want to find fault, you can. To help everyone, including yourself, take the time with the person sending you to be sure you both understand and agree upon your task. Ask for these specifics: what are you expected to do; what results are you responsible for; are written reports required; what determines when your task is completed; and to whom do you report?

I have seen sad outcomes when project managers are thrown at problem projects without a plan for the assistance. On several occasions, one project manager was sent on an emergency basis just so his home department would be seen as willing and capable of swift action with able resources. While admirable, the lack of a plan led to less than useful help.

A visiting project manager's attitude makes the difference. The best response is to show up and behave in a manner that says, "I'm here to help you be successful." Faultfinding keeps you at a distance from, and uncommitted to, anything the project is doing. Once you offer help, you are getting your professional fingerprints on the project and confidence and competence are required to see it through. When you are positive and take charge, you expose yourself to criticism from others who will assess your performance. It's analogous to the need for a product to be of good quality for it to gain acceptance. Studies show that if you try a new product and you don't like it, you'll tell eight other people about your negative experience. However, if you like it you will tell only three other people.

A $10 million project that I was called upon to help was five months from startup, overrunning its budget and getting bad press in the company. I found the project manager at his desk with a foot-tall stack of change orders from the contractors. He also said the startup was going to be late by at least a month. I spent several days at the site talking, listening and observing to identify the problems. Among them, a design engineering firm new to big projects provided sub-par construction documents. In addition, a lump-sum contracting approach on a fast-track project and a less than adequate field office staff complicated matters. The plant organized and staffed the troubled project like they were re-paving the parking lot rather than building a $10 million facility.

My recommendation was to focus energy on completing the construction and do what was required to assure a good startup. Companies don't like overruns or being late, but an installation that doesn't work is fatal. A good startup will buy forgiveness for other project sins in many companies. An alternative was to shut the project down and get it into sync with better engineering, claims cleaned up and an appropriate staff in place.

I saw other shortcomings on this specific project. The plant management was paralyzed by the cost overrun, since this was the first one in five years at that plant. This tells us something about the corporate culture of rewards for favorable variances (actual results better than the target). Also, everyone needed to share mutual objectives with the consequences understood. Over those five years, how much investment went into assets that didn't provide shareholder value?

## Review process...

A relatively new feature of process projects is the hazardous operations review. This is directed at making the facility safe to operate and maintain. A series of what-if questions leads a team through the design, looking for flaws.

A few of the projects I've been involved with required an even more basic review aimed at common sense, which isn't always so common. In one project we were mating a large diesel engine to a pump. It wasn't until we were into construction that someone thought to ask if the direction of rotation of both machines matched; fortunately they did. Several years earlier at the same plant, a new steam driven turbine drove a fan backwards, which led to costly repairs. Because even incorrectly connected centrifugal units will move fluids, I would bet that a number of industrial fans have been running backwards for years.

The lesson I learned is that the role of the project manager is to step back with a few smart people and review what is being planned with a simple questioning approach. Does what we are doing make sense? Are we comfortable with how the work is progressing? Are there any looming black clouds or land mines? Can we visually walk through the plans and work done to date and see the positive outcomes?

You can invent your own questions. The need is to get past the details to see if the ship is still on course and whether it will make it to port. This is a challenge for most engineers who get into the details and love it there.

The business vice-president who was responsible for two of my projects joked with me that he was the captain steering the business toward the far sunny horizon. I responded that our project team had a person hanging out of a forward porthole looking for mines and torpedoes and shouting directions back to the engine room because we had disconnected the steering mechanism from the bridge so the captain would think he was still in control of our direction but in reality couldn't steer us into disaster.

That vice-president also led me to understand my role as a project manager in our company's culture. I thought my role was that of a circus ringmaster who organized and presented the acts according to the standard script. Actually, I was the zookeeper calming the elephants so they wouldn't get excited, stomp around and hurt someone. Think about your project in terms of internal and external requirements. Who will do what, when and how much and what should the review process be?

## Safety behavior...

During the Procter & Gamble startup and expansion of the Pampers operation in Michigan in the 1950s, a lesson emerged concerning how to motivate workers to improve safety.

Initially, the Pampers production lines involved complicated pieces of equipment with many pinch points and hot spots. Accidents involved cut or mashed fingers and burns on hands and forearms. We used P & G's traditional safety programs in this brand-new facility without measurable success. They were ineffective because they were designed for established operations and experienced employees that we did not have. Employee attitude was another contributing factor. In the outdoor culture they came from, scars were the badges of honor for doing risky things. Using safety equipment was considered unmanly and a source of ridicule from their buddies.

One day at a safety meeting, where we cursed the darkness for the umpteenth time, a foreman said we should shift the focus to the employees' activities away from the plant. He said the program should underline the negative effects of accidents on the employees' time at home and when they were hunting, fishing and snowmobiling. A relatively simple program was developed that mainly displayed several serious questions: "Who is going to cut up your meat at dinner when you can't? Can you cast left-handed? Can you hunt one-handed?"

The outcome of this new effort was a dramatic reduction in accidents. Appealing to the lifestyle of the workforce and putting the "what's in it for me" answers at the top of the list was an early example of the behavior-based safety approach. The philosophy behind it can work for other issues, too.

## Selection process...

Most companies have a procedure for making a selection among competing design engineers, suppliers or construction contractors. There are the "musts" that a potential firm must meet or they don't make the list. For those that pass the "musts," there is a list of "wants" that describe other areas and assign weights to each "want" in proportion to its importance on the project's outcome. After an interview and perhaps acquiring some other specific data, the scores are tabulated and a winner is determined. This process sounds simple and straightforward, but my experience differs in several cases.

On one particular boiler project, we had developed a selection process. But, in the middle of one design firm's interview our operations vice-president asked their lead engineer if they had met before. "Yes," replied the engineer, "we both captained sailboats in several of the same races on Puget Sound." We had found our designer!

In another instance of contractor selection, the plant manager approved the selection format and a list of four contractors. But when the process selected a contractor, he informed us that he didn't want the one chosen. Why, he was asked, did he allow the contractor on the list? He said that he never thought the contractor would be selected. We talked him into using the selected contractor, who performed well. We were strongly motivated to make him successful as we believed in the process. Had we not established understanding and acceptance of the process by the accountable manager prior to using it, we would have created a different challenge.

Another lesson I relearned is that you should not use your project to prove that a design firm, supplier or contractor is capable. That also applies if you are seeking a supply-design-build combination. If the firms have not worked together before, you are embarking into unknown territory.

## Sexual harassment...

The construction industry has many examples of sexual harassment in its macho culture. We must improve.

A consultant who worked with Washington State Ferries a few years ago suggested an excellent approach. She said the golden rule was wrong. If you are a macho redneck harasser, treating others as you would have them treat you makes no sense. It's guaranteed to get you and your employer into trouble. The "platinum rule" was her recommendation: treat others as they would treat themselves. This sensitive solution is obvious. Doing it is a stretch for some as their insensitivity gets in the way.

It's hard to change attitudes during a project's brief life. All firms at all levels are vulnerable. I have witnessed inappropriate behavior by management people as well as hourly craftspeople. No organization is immune.

## Solving problems...

The procedures and systems that companies use to run capital projects can achieve excellent results as long as pivotal issues fall into place, and project participants have the skill to reach into their toolboxes and pull out the right tool at the right time. My experience is that things don't usually happen that way. There will always be problems.

The management group may think they have the best solutions, but there is demonstrated evidence that the people who do the work know more about the problems and may provide excellent remedies if they are asked. I saw examples of involvement of journeymen in problem solving where good outcomes occurred.

In one case, it was discovered that an unusually high number of work hours were incurred cutting electrical cable to length for wire runs. An investigation found that the wire reels were badly located during delivery in an area where the cable, as it was unreeled, had to be awkwardly snaked around some obstructions. The measurements were inexact which resulted in more work and more scrap wire when the cable was pulled into place. The delivery truck driver had chosen the easiest place to unload them. The reason the problem wasn't recognized earlier speaks to our comfort with the status quo.

A requirement for generating ideas is that you must understand the problem you are trying to fix. Years ago on a United Airlines flight, I recognized Richard Ferris, then United's president, standing in the galley watching the flight attendants prepare the lunch trays. He told me that he wasn't taking a busman's holiday but rather he had many complaints from United employees about the inefficient galley layout in a new generation passenger plane. I don't know the outcome of his effort, but I'll bet he learned the facts and the employees respected his direct involvement.

# Startup...

One of the pivotal details that every project must plan for is the transition from construction to full operation of the facility. Early in the project, while everyone is enjoying the honeymoon, the distant startup is not seriously addressed. The schedule most often shows a December startup, which is unrealistic since folks from every participating organization are (or want to be) on vacation, the weather is lousy and the prevailing holiday spirit is distracting.

About six months before the startup, a key person from the project and the new facility operations manager should go through the startup plan and identify what must be done and in what sequence. Add names later. Check prior company startups, both plans for and critiques of the event. Better yet, interview some players from successful startups and poor startups. You probably will learn more from the marginal ones.

There is much written about commissioning, training, startup and initial operation. I needn't reproduce it here, as the checklists are available elsewhere. Who is in charge at any given moment is critical as no leadership or dual leadership equals failure.

A simple and effective startup technique was used on a recovery boiler project at Scott Paper Company in Everett, Washington in 1974. A baseball bat, the so-called "startup stick," was painted several eye-catching colors. The project manager had the bat 24 hours a day during the project's responsible period. Project people pushed buttons, opened valves, directed work. Operations people observed, asked questions, took notes.

When fuel went to the boiler, the startup stick went into the hands of the utilities manager. Project folks followed operators who now ran the show. It worked well. The details of planning and updating progress were all there, but the symbolism of the startup stick, representing power, a sense of urgency and responsibility, made the right things happen.

## Success factors ...

A challenging subject in project work is the development of meaningful success factors to measure production, product quality, safety results and other issues. Having a disparate group of project participants develop, understand and accept each factor, including the gradations around the factors, is often difficult.

The culture of the company is the single most influential factor followed by the desires of the person who is identified as responsible for the investment. A truism by a Chevron engineer expressed it well, "Behavior is perfectly aligned with the consequences in place." The setting of success factors will be driven by the desire for reward and the avoidance of pain.

If management rewards favorable results greater than the target, then "under-promise and over-perform" is the criteria for success. If the reward system is geared to coming closest to the target, then realistic targets should be set but be aware that the system may drive some unjustified spending if a cost underrun is anticipated. In the case of one of my employers, the rule was never go back to the board of directors for additional money. In this company, estimates were generous, spending rose to meet available funds, and the mills got their bells and whistles. Everyone was happy, except the company never led their industry in return on assets.

In every company I worked for, the one overriding success factor was the expectation that the new installation function well. Delays or cost overruns would be forgiven if the system met the production volume and quality targets. If the new facility didn't work well, the other yardsticks were irrelevant.

# Time...

Time is the one factor that influences every outcome. Unfortunately, not everyone gives time its full potential for producing poor results.

Think about a project and its organization as a temporary manufacturing effort producing one item, the constructed facility. Thousands of big and small decisions shape the outcome. A principal difference between good and bad judgment is knowing how much time, and energy, to put into making a specific decision.

One project manager decided he didn't have time to resolve change orders as the project unfolded. He chose to defer all claims discussions until after startup. When the project was completed, a long and expensive settlement resulted, negotiated by people who were never involved in the project. The original project participants had moved on to other assignments.

A project needs an issue resolution process aimed at settling differences in a timely way. If you try to invent a resolution process later, when you are fighting, it will be doubly difficult. Allow a few days for agreement between the parties who are at odds with each other. If the dispute is not resolved, move it up the organization. However, should too many differences move up the chain, managers will question the skills and motivations of those under them.

A time deadline creates a sense of urgency and keeps people focused on getting started up promptly so benefits produced by the project are realized sooner. On projects that generate income, this is a payoff for everyone. Use posters and have the countdown displayed on memos and screensavers. On one project, I handed out one-ounce silver coins with the message: "This coin is your reminder that the objective of this project is to make money. Also, let it be your decision-maker.

If you have a difficult decision between two acceptable options, flip the coin and move on. Time is our enemy!"

In my early education as a new hire, I learned an interesting lesson in deciding how much time to spend on an issue. It came as a result of a vice-president's question to a group of us: "If the boss asked you the height of the stack on the boiler house, how would you respond?" One person said that with a transit and surveyor's rod he could use similar triangles to calculate the height. Another offered that there was probably a drawing of the stack in the engineering office.

While both these ideas would work, the vice-president replied that the correct first response was to ask the boss why he wanted to know, how accurate should the data be and when did he need it. If the boss said his wife had asked him out of curiosity, then a five-minute answer would be appropriate. If, however, there was a new federal requirement for structures over 100 feet to have flashing strobe lights (costing several thousand dollars) the answer needed some precise research.

The vice-president pointed out that time is the enemy, not knowledge or money. He said that providing hundred dollar answers to five cent questions is one of the principal burdens faced by business. "We tend to overreact to the bosses we encounter and want to give the best we can do, but that's not always the right use of our limited time and resources. Don't forget the lesson when you are the boss, either. It's partly your responsibility to avoid having your people waste time on developing detailed information that has no benefit in exactness."

Time is often wasted in meetings. Agendas, strong discussion leaders and ground rules help. If questions were asked with one or two sentences and answered as succinctly, much time would be saved. Another technique used by a plant manager I knew was to have no chairs in the conference room. That definitely sped up the meetings.

One final point: in a contract estimate, we always include contingency, escalation and unlisted items. Do we ever show any similar allowances in the time schedules?

# About the Author...

Paul F. Snare's career spans forty years, primarily managing capital projects with Procter & Gamble, International Playtex, Scott Paper Company and the Weyerhaeuser Company. He has a civil engineering degree and an MBA, both from Cornell University. He is a registered professional engineer in Washington and New York. Paul and his wife, Louise, reside in the state of Washington.

www.ingramcontent.com/pod-product-compliance
Lightning Source LLC
Chambersburg PA
CBHW030856180526
45163CB00004B/1597